# How to Buy a Horse

## without being taken for a ride

Peter Brown MRCVS

Sponsored by
Strongid*-P

**HENSTON**

*Trade Mark

First published 1993

© Henston Ltd, 1993

ISBN 1 85054 092 6

The opinions and advice given in this guide are those of the author, a practicing veterinary surgeon, and Henston editorial staff. They do not necessarily reflect the views of the Royal College of Veterinary Surgeons or of any other professional association.

Henston Ltd, The Chequers, 2 Church Street, High Wycombe, Bucks, England

Printed and bound by Brier Press Ltd, High Wycombe, Bucks

Cover design by CBA & Associates Ltd

Cover photograph by James Nash shows Kady, 12 year old gelding, 14.1 h.h., half Arab Chestnut.

**HENSTON**

# Contents

# Foreword

Purchasing a horse is a big step which can have serious short and long term implications. A bad buy not only means a financial loss but may also give rise to a long term commitment to an animal which does not match the purpose for which it was purchased.

The advice contained in this book has been prepared by a veterinary surgeon in equine practice in the UK. Every day contact with the horse-owning public has given the author first hand knowledge of the many pitfalls awaiting the prospective horse owner, and he is ideally placed to pass on this knowledge and experience in a down-to-earth, jargon-free way which will be readily understood even by the least experienced horse person.

By all means buy a horse, but don't get taken for a ride!

Jim Evans MRCVS & Allan Henderson BVM&S MRCVS
EDITORS

# Acknowledgements

The author and publishers gratefully acknowledge the support of Pfizer (UK) Ltd, the makers of Strongid*-P, who have generously sponsored production of this first edition.

The words of 'A horse, A horse' were first published in Horse & Hound and are reprinted with the permission of the Editor and of the author.

*Trade Mark

# Preface

Thank you for buying this guide—I am sure you will not regret the small investment you have made. If used properly, its contents could save you hundreds, even thousands, of pounds and could prevent much disappointment and heartache in the future.

Buying your first horse or pony should be a great thrill and pleasure. For many, however, it becomes an arduous and frustrating experience that too often results in a poor choice of animal. This need not be the case.

My aim is to steer you through the obstacles and hazards you will meet at all stages of the buying process; to prevent you from making bad decisions; and to show you how to be objective in choosing an animal suited to the purposes you intend. The horse world is littered with phrases and terms that mean very little and yet, to the uninitiated, can sound very impressive and important. The guide is designed to be as 'jargon free' as possible to overcome this problem.

As with many businesses, there are many rogues and dealers in the horse trade out to make a quick buck. Make sure you are not one of their unsuspecting victims. Follow each stage of the guide and you will not go wrong. Do not take shortcuts—you will only live to regret them. The details laid out here are not 'pie in the sky' ideas, they are practical methods derived from experience that can be readily put into practice.

The saying 'a little knowledge is a dangerous thing' is something always to bear in mind when purchasing a horse or pony. Many people are persuaded to part with their hard earned money because they think they know what they are doing. Don't fall into this trap. Seek guidance when it is needed.

Peter Brown, 1993

# A horse, A horse!

I want a horse.
A special horse, of course.
A horse of quality and speed,
strong of limb, of fiery breed,
whose ears will cock and nostrils crack
as he strives to catch the flying pack
with 18 stone on his back.

*Chorus*
I know just the very horse for you, brown, or black, or bay.
I had him in this very yard and sold him yesterday.

Put out the feelers.
Ring up the dealers.
Drive 300 miles on a foggy day
to find the man has gone away
but he's left 'the Boy' who isn't 20 shillings in the pound,
the horse who's 15.3 and quite unsound:
for this he wants three thousand pound?

*Chorus*

Black despair, pull out hair.
I try a horse (amazing bold)
But 'mind, he takes a little hold'.
For half an hour he nearly, but not quite, runs away;
what a horse! what power! hooray! hooray!
then I have to get off and push for
the rest of the day.

*Chorus*

No more smiles;
travelled miles;
seen horses coloured black to grey,
but none are *ever* what they say.
I now know that 16.2 means 15.3 and 8 means a generous 12,
that's why it would be nice if just once someone
told me the truth before I drove miles to try it:
then I might buy it.

R W F Poole

# Chapter 1

# Deciding whether to buy

**General considerations**

**Cost considerations**
    **Purchase price**
    **Tack**
    **Accommodation**
    **Equipment**
    **Bedding**
    **Feeding**
    **Farriery**
    **Veterinary costs**
        **and health care**
    **Transport**
    **Insurance**

The decision to buy a horse or pony must never be made on the spur of the moment. The problems of finding a suitable animal can be small when compared to the problems and cost of upkeep. It is vital that *all* aspects of horse ownership are carefully thought through.

In buying a horse or pony, you are committing yourself to the care and maintenance of that animal while you own it. Unlike a car or camera, you cannot just put the animal to one side and ignore it.

Horses and ponies come in all shapes and sizes. Many people are familiar with the Thelwell cartoons—when looking for a suitable animal, you will realise just how perceptive they actually are. Tall ones, short ones, thin ones, fat ones, shaggy ones, and so on. The choice is yours. Clearly, the animal you choose must be suited to the environment in which it is to be kept. The conditions needed by a Thoroughbred are not the same as those for a New Forest pony.

The first serious question to consider is for whom the animal is being bought. Remember, growing children will outgrow a pony just as they will outgrow shoes and clothes. If you are not planning to keep the pony for the rest of its life, then the resale value of the animal may be important, and this may in turn influence at the outset which animal you buy. Ponies and horses can also be outgrown in terms of experience as the novice rider progresses. It is important to think ahead to future needs and to consider what the animal will be expected to do now and in the longer term.

Realistic alternatives to buying do exist and should be seriously considered, especially if you have any doubt about what size and type of animal you require. If your available time for horse riding is very limited (perhaps you can only ride at weekends or occasionally during the week), then it may be more appropriate and cost effective to rent horses or ponies on an occasional basis from a good local riding establishment. This will obviously limit the type of animal you can ride and restrict scope for competitive work. However, it eliminates the need for you to provide the regular exercise necessary to keep the animal fit and the need to be responsible for daily stable management.

An alternative to buying your own animal is to take a pony or horse on loan. Loans can be short term or long term. A loan avoids the high initial cost of purchase or the need to buy tack. It is, however, limiting in that the owner may request the animal back at some stage. With any loan arrangement, it is essential (even with friends) to establish *in writing* at the outset who is responsible for the farrier's costs, vet bills, insurance and so on.

## Points to consider before deciding to purchase

If you can answer yes to all the questions below, you have passed the first hurdle to horse ownership.

- ❐ Can you or someone in the family you can trust give to the horse the time needed for feeding, watering, grooming and exercising?
- ❐ Do you have an adequate amount of land and suitable accommodation available the year round?
- ❐ If you are leasing land, is there anything to prohibit you keeping a horse?
- ❐ Do you have access to suitable transport?
- ❐ Can you afford the vets' fees if the horse is ill or goes lame?
- ❐ Can you afford to feed the horse properly?
- ❐ Have you taken into account the fact that horses age and may need special care and medication?
- ❐ Is there anyone who can cope if you fall ill?

Having decided that buying is the option for you, it is necessary to consider *all* the costs that will be involved. These can be summarised as follows:

# Cost considerations

### Purchase price
The initial price paid is only one aspect of the total cost. While the price can be high, it is, of course, a one off payment. Clearly, the price of horses and ponies varies tremendously, so it is vital that you set an upper limit over which you will not go (very much like buying a house). That said, it is worth looking at animals slightly above your price range since there may be considerable scope for bargaining over the price.

In some cases, tack and other ancillary equipment (such as grooming gear, rugs, travelling boots, etc.) may be offered or included in the cost of the purchase. While such incentives can be very tempting, it is essential to assess the quality and condition of all such equipment and whether it is really what you want. This is especially the case with expensive items such as the saddle. You may find that some of the equipment fits poorly or is in need of expensive repairs or, indeed, may not even be suited to your requirements.

### Tack
The animal cannot be ridden without tack (saddlery). There is no point in paying as much as possible for the best animal and then having no money left to buy good quality tack. A poorly fitting, uncomfortable saddle will ruin the best horse and make life a misery for horse and owner alike.

When calculating costs, tack must be included in the reckoning. As with people, not all horses and ponies are standard sizes—extra expenditure may be necessary on special items, even made-to-measure equipment could be required. Care taken in selecting good quality tack that suits your personal riding requirements and fits the animal well will ensure durability and potentially a lifetime of service.

Investing in second-hand equipment can be financially rewarding providing measures are taken to ensure that the gear is in good order. However, do not take risks—costly and even dangerous mistakes can be made if cheap or damaged saddlery is bought.

Certain basic items of tack will be required and these can be summarised as follows:

● *Saddle*

The single most expensive item of tack. There are various shapes and styles available but in most cases a general purpose (GP) saddle is most suitable for general riding activities. A poorly fitting saddle can do untold damage to a horse or pony's back, so always use an expert saddler. Do not depend on luck.

● *Saddle leathers and stirrup irons*

The leathers will stretch as they are broken in and they should be swapped from side to side occasionally since more weight is generally put on the left side due to mounting. The stirrup irons need to be checked for fit since if they are too small the foot can become jammed and if too large the foot may pass right through and become trapped.

● *Girth*

This keeps the saddle in position. Girths are available in a variety of materials and styles. Beware particularly of rubbing which can cause soreness or discomfort for the animal.

● *Bridle (including bit and reins)*

As with the saddle, it is important that the bridle chosen fits the animal concerned. A bit is also required—numerous styles and types of bit are available but most are relevant only to the expert. In most cases a simple snaffle bit will be required but you should seek advice in determining the most suitable bit type for your particular animal and needs. The bit needs to be measured against the animals mouth to ensure an adequate fit thereby avoiding damage to the mouth. The reins can be made of various materials, leather being a common choice.

● *Numnah*

An inexpensive but important piece of tack which provides a protective pad between the saddle and the animal's back. Since it can harbour infection it is probably sensible to buy new.

The choice of tack is vast and numerous additional pieces of saddlery are available. It is not within the scope of this book to discuss the pros and cons of different types of saddlery but much useful information is contained in other relevant books. See Appendix 6, Suggested further reading.

**Accommodation**

Having acquired a horse or pony it is vital to have made arrangements for accommodating the animal. This may be undertaken by yourself if you own some land or are able to rent suitable pasture. Alternatively, you may make use of existing riding establishments where facilities and equipment are provided.

● *Grass keep*

It is possible to keep horses and ponies permanently at grass and thus avoid the need for stabling. Many of the native pony breeds (e.g. Dartmoor, New Forest) and some of the hardier horse breeds are very well suited to this type of management. Since good grass will not be available throughout the year, some supplementary feeding at grass will be necessary.

Maintaining the quality of the pasture is very important and so dividing the land into a number of paddocks (fenced areas) is ideal to enable areas to be rested. This can be achieved either by permanent fencing or with mobile electric fencing. Conditions in fields can become very difficult in winter with mud and flooding, especially around gateways.

Other potential disadvantages can be problems with catching the animal and keeping the animal clean. Sound fencing is vital, not only to help maintain the pasture but also to prevent the animal wandering.

Security from theft or assult is another factor to consider (horse rustling is still big business, even in this day and age). Fencing needs to be safe—post and rail fencing is ideal but expensive; barbed wire is widely used but is one of the more common causes of injury.

With grass keep, it is still necessary to provide a source of fresh water. It is usually desirable to provide a simple shelter to act as a windbreak and shelter from rain.

● *Stabling*

Many new owners will choose to stable their horse or pony for at least some time during the year. Regardless of the materials from which the stable is constructed, it should serve to provide a clean and safe environment for the animal. The space required will depend on the size of the animal concerned but, in approximate terms, a pony will need a stable about 10' x 12' (3m x 3.5m) whilst an average sized horse will require a stable in the region of 12' x 14' (3.5m x 4.5m).

Numerous other matters must be considered when constructing stabling—particularly ventilation, water supply (automatic versus buckets), door width and height, flooring and drainage, electricity supply, mangers and rings for feeding, convenience of bedding disposal and so on. These considerations will apply also to people converting existing buildings for use as stabling.

● *Existing Riding Establishments*

Many new purchasers will not have access to their own land and will need to make use of existing riding establishments. These may simply provide stables and land on which the horse can be kept as outlined above but without the responsibility for the provision and upkeep of fencing, pasture or buildings; you, however, remain responsible for the daily feeding and management of the animal itself. At the other end of the spectrum, some establishments provide a wide range of equipment and facilities (e.g. indoor and outdoor schooling areas, cross-country courses, qualified riding instructors and managers, etc.) and can provide full livery facilities (i.e. take full responsibility for the daily feeding and management of the animal). Every variation between these two extremes exists and the weekly cost will reflect the precise nature of the facility or service provided.

## Equipment

Depending on where the animal is kept, other items of equipment may be needed. These may include the following:

- *Tack cleaning equipment*—sponge, saddle soap, saddle oil, metal polish, chamois leather, etc.
- *Grooming kit*—hoof pick, body brush, stiff (Dandy) brush, curry comb, mane comb, hoof oil, etc.
- *Rugs*—numerous types are now available made of a wide variety of materials. These need to fit properly to prevent slipping and rubbing.
- *Bandages*—stable, exercise, and tail bandages.
- *Basic first aid kit*—cotton wool, scissors, disinfectant, wound cream or powder, dressings, etc.
- *Boots*—e.g. travelling boots, over-reach boots, tendon boots, etc.
- *Riders' clothing*—as well as equiping the animal, it is important to equip yourself with safe and appropriate riding wear.

## Bedding

A variety of bedding materials are now used for horses and ponies. Those most commonly seen are straw and wood shavings but shredded paper is increasingly popular and peat is also used. More recently, synthetic permeable floors have become available that reduce or even eliminate the need for other types of bedding material.

Straw remains immensely popular because it is cheap and readily available. However, many of the breathing problems seen in stabled animals are almost certainly due to the use of dusty bedding and feed materials in enclosed poorly ventilated environments. From this point of view, straw is a poor choice of bedding material. Furthermore, you may purchase an animal that is developing or has already developed a sensitivity or allergy to dust in which case the use of dust free bedding materials will be a necessity.

Wood shavings and shredded paper are now comparable in price but are certainly considerably more costly than straw in the longer term. The synthetic floors mentioned above are costly to install but can be very cost effective in the long term if they wear well.

## Feeding

The feeding requirements of individual animals will vary enormously with the type of animal concerned. The requirements of most horses during the summer months can be met from grass; indeed, with some animals, especially ponies, it may be necessary to restrict their access to grass to avoid them developing the serious condition of laminitis. If there is a shortage of grass (e.g. due to overgrazing or a very dry summer), it may be necessary to supplement the grazing with conserved forage (e.g. hay) and/or concentrates. The need for supplementary feeding during the summer will also be influenced by the amount of work (exercise) the animal is being asked to do.

As grass availability decreases during the autumn and winter months, it will be necessary to introduce other feed materials. Hay is likely to make up the bulk of the feed. The need for concentrates (e.g. barley, oats, sugar beet pulp) will depend on the type of animal involved and the level of exercise undertaken.

Many owners make feeding unnecessarily complicated by using a multitude of different feed stuffs. This can be readily overcome by using proprietary brands of concentrates containing a well-balanced feed mixture that is formulated to meet the needs of the animal.

The cost of feeding on a weekly basis will clearly vary with season, level of exercise and the animal's size. It is an unavoidable and costly component of the maintenance and upkeep of a horse or pony and should never be under-estimated.

## Farriery

Trimming the feet and shoeing will need to be undertaken on a regular basis (every 4-8 weeks). It is essential to keep the feet in good order if the animal is going to do the work asked of it. Remember the adage 'no foot, no horse'. The costs of shoeing have increased considerably in recent years and the difficulties in finding and keeping a good farrier should not be underestimated.

## Veterinary costs and health care

● *Illness and injury*

Veterinary bills arising from injury or illness can be substantial and unpredictable. Sadly, horses can injure themselves indoors and out, whether working or resting. They are also susceptible to diseases over which you may have little or no control.

● *Health care*

Some conditions can be readily prevented. All horses and ponies can be routinely vaccinated to protect them against tetanus and equine influenza.

Tetanus is a very serious, potentially fatal, condition caused by a toxin produced by a specific type of bacterium *(Clostridium tetani)*. This organism is common in the environment and most usually enters the animal through a wound, often a tiny unseen puncture. Tetanus is entirely avoidable by vaccination. It is not a contagious disease (i.e. it is not transmitted from one horse to another) but all unvaccinated animals are at risk.

Influenza is a less serious condition than tetanus but can be a cause of considerable distress to the animal. It is also important since it is a contagious condition. Since horses and ponies are often kept in groups and taken to shows, there is considerable scope for the spread of infection. Vaccination of all horses and ponies against influenza can help to keep the threat of a major outbreak (epidemic) at a low level.

You should discuss these important diseases with your vet as soon as possible after purchase, especially if there is a question mark over whether or not the animal has been vaccinated previously.

Another important but avoidable cause of ill health is worm infestation. Regular worming (or more correctly de-worming) using special types of drug called anthelmintics or wormers will help to prevent the build up of large numbers of worms in your animal. It is again important to discuss with your veterinary surgeon how often you should worm and with what drug—but as a general guide this should be carried out every 6-8 weeks throughout the year. Every year horses and ponies become severely ill and even die as a consequence of owners failing to take the threat from worm damage seriously— *Don't be one of those caught out!*

## Transport

To gain maximum pleasure from owning a horse or pony, it is often necessary to travel to shows or different areas for leisure riding. This can be restricted if you have no form of transportation. The two types of transport available are horse boxes, or trailers designed to be towed behind a powered vehicle. Horse boxes tend to be more stable and safer than trailers but are an expensive investment and have limited alternative uses. Trailers can be very good but must be of sound design; it is also important to check the vehicle you intend to use to tow with is up to the job. Remember, an average horse will weigh in the region of 500kg.

## Insurance

It is vital to obtain insurance cover against accidents involving other people or vehicles. You would also be wise to insure against vets bills, loss of use of the animal, and accidental death or humane destruction.

*It is essential to read all insurance policies very carefully*—make sure you understand what you are covered against. For example, an animal may be rendered unfit to ride but may not be suffering to the point where a vet would advise euthanasia on humane grounds; in such a case, the cover required is that for 'loss of use'. If you have any doubts about the nature of the cover provided you should immediately consult the insurance company or broker concerned.

Insurance cover is considered in more detail in Appendix 5.

*Golden rule: When buying a horse or pony, consider* all *the costs involved, not just the cost of the animal itself.*

# Chapter 2

# From whom and where to buy

**Private sale**

**Auctions and markets**

**Dealers**

**Riding schools**

**Breeders and training centres**

**Rescue centres**

The saying 'you pay for what you get' is certainly relevant when buying a horse or pony. A good quality animal will command a considerable premium. Many people hope to find a real bargain and, indeed, such bargains do occasionally come along. However, the chances of being in the right place at the right time are small, and unless you are very experienced in horse dealing, such an approach cannot be recommended. For every true bargain, there will be dozens that are anything but a bargain.

There are many sources of ponies and horses, all with their pros and cons. However, the basic approach to all of them is the same. Tread with caution and follow the advice outlined later in this guide.

## Private Sale

Many animals are advertised in national and local magazines and newspapers. The descriptions can look very appealing. Of course, if an animal sounds a promising candidate, go and have a look. But do so objectively. Ask yourself why the horse or pony is being sold and don't always believe what you are told. Beware of the 'quick sale—owner going abroad' scam. Also remember if an animal is a long way from your home, it is much more difficult simply to return it.

Some apparently private ads will in fact be dealers so again be aware. When you call in response to an advert purporting to be a private sale, make reference only to 'the pony' or 'the horse'—if the person is a dealer, he or she will have to ask 'to which horse or pony are you referring?'.

It is often worth talking to other local horse owners or your vet or farrier since you can sometimes get a sounding on a suspicious sale before you even look at the animal.

## Auctions and markets

These sources cannot be recommended for first time buyers. Many very unsuitable animals are 'off-loaded' through such places. Returning horses, even under warranty, can be a real nightmare that is best avoided. It is also very difficult to have animals vetted at such places before committing yourself to purchase. It is very easy to get carried away at auctions because things happen so fast. It is also easy to bid for animals for sympathetic reasons which may commit you to an animal of no value to yourself, however good your intentions were. *Be warned*!

## Dealers

There are good dealers and there are bad dealers. As with second hand car sales, the cowboys are there to con you. Some dealers will give you nothing but trouble, so before parting with any money, ask around the area about such people. It is often possible to pick up useful information that can save you much hassle later. If you do approach a dealer, do not allow yourself to be intimidated (some can appear quite threatening) and *do not part with any money* before making certain that the horse is definitely the one for you by following the advice given in the rest of this guide.

## Riding schools

On some occasions, you may be offered a horse or pony at your local riding centre. It may be an animal you have ridden and know very well. These can be good opportunities to pick up a sound animal. However, you should still follow *all* the suggestions laid out in this guide since you may overlook major problems (do not be blinkered by the fact that you think you know the animal).

## Breeders and training centres

Breeders are generally a source of youngsters (foals, yearlings and two year olds) and are certainly not for the novice first time buyer. In some centres, animals may be broken and brought on ready for sale. Novice or inexperienced riders should be very wary of buying novice young horses.

## Rescue centres

It is very easy to become emotional when seeing the conditions from which some horses and ponies are rescued. However, it is one thing to provide a suitable home for a rescued pony but quite another to expect to buy a suitable working animal from such sources. Remember, when looking at horses and ponies, you must always remain objective. Avoid spur of the moment and emotional decisions at all costs.

To summarise, you should approach all sources of horses and ponies objectively with a view to finding the type of animal you consider suitable for your needs. Do not allow yourself to be carried away by irrational or emotive influences. Under no circumstances allow yourself to be cajoled into making a decision regarding purchase before you are good and ready.

*Golden Rule: When buying a horse or pony, never trust anybody, even your best-friend!*

# Chapter 3

# Choosing the right horse or pony

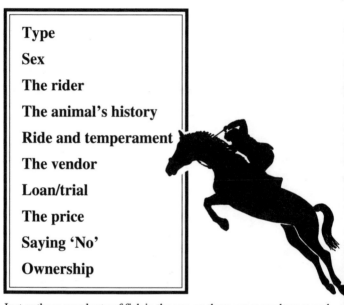

Type

Sex

The rider

The animal's history

Ride and temperament

The vendor

Loan/trial

The price

Saying 'No'

Ownership

Just as there are plenty of fish in the sea, so there are many horses and ponies to choose from. It is very easy to see and fall in love with the first animal that you look at without considering its potential problems. Remember, the theme throughout so far has been objective consideration. Consider each of the points noted below during the decision process.

## Type of animal

As mentioned earlier, horses and ponies come in all shapes and sizes and have very variable temperaments. When considering a particular animal, it is essential to consider the conditions under which it will be kept (e.g. a Thoroughbred type is unlikely to be suited to a permanent pasture situation) and the type of work it is intended to do (e.g. hacking, jumping, eventing, driving, western style, dressage, gymkhanas, etc.).

## Sex

The majority of male horses will have been gelded (castrated) and will, therefore, have no breeding potential. Stallions are generally not a practical proposition for inexperienced owners. Mares can be used for breeding—this can be an advantage should the animal cease to be useful for riding purposes for any reason. However, the temperament of some mares can be rather variable. For example, when they are in season (that is the period during which the mare will allow a stallion to mate with her), some mares will be erratic and unpredictable in their behaviour.

## The rider

It is vital to consider who will actually be riding the animal. The competence and confidence of the rider must be assessed accurately. Many horses are described as 'a difficult ride' or 'not for novices' and such warnings should be heeded. If several people are to use the horse, then the riding abilities of all concerned must be considered. Riding is a process of education for both horse and rider. *But*, many a good horse has been ruined by an inexperienced or poor rider. It is unwise, therefore, to consider purchase until a reasonable level of riding competence has been achieved.

## The animal's history

Try to find out about the animal's past. In many cases it is difficult to accurately or reliably establish a detailed history of the earlier life of the animal you are considering. Beware of the vendor who says 'the papers are in Ireland' or 'I'll send the papers on later' or 'he is vaccinated but I don't have a vaccination certificate'. Many such statements should be treated with suspicion. Furthermore, many vendors will make claims about a horse that are impossible to substantiate at the time, if at all. Factors such as the worming history of the animal are obviously very important but can be difficult to establish—use common sense and look at the environment from which the horse is coming; consider whether it is overgrazed ('horsesick') pasture; look at the condition of other horses at the same place. Life is made more tricky when a horse has recently been imported (e.g. from Ireland or Belgium). Many of the problems that cannot be determined at the time of purchase can be covered by a warranty (see Chapter 6).

## Ride and temperament

However ideal a horse or pony may seem when looked at from the ground, it is vital that the ride is equally appealing since an uncomfortable ride can put you off riding for life. It is a bit like buying a second hand car with great bodywork but in need of new suspension or a new engine. It is also essential to ride the animal prior to purchase to try and assess riding temperament and to look out for breathing or lameness problems that become apparent during exercise.

## The vendor

Study the vendor as well as the animal. A shrewd dealer can make even the most run-down dead beat seem like a good buy. Don't be gullible and don't be forced into making a decision before you are good and ready.

## Loaning or trialing the animal

You may have the opportunity to have the animal on trial for a short period. This can be very worthwhile but the legal implications must be considered. While on loan, nothing should be done to the animal (e.g. changing shoes, clipping, mane or tail pulling) until a decision to buy has been made. Should anything be done to the animal without the express consent of the vendor (make certain that consent is in writing), then the vendor can deem this to represent 'purchase' and refuse return of the animal. This holds true even if the animal is in urgent need of, for example, new shoes. Any problem points should be sorted out with the legal owner (the vendor at this stage) *before* the animal is accepted on trial. You would be strongly advised to provide some form of insurance cover during the trial period since accidents can, of course, happen at any time.

## The price

An obvious question that should always be asked is whether the vendor is asking a fair price. As with anything, a horse or pony is only worth as much as any one is prepared to pay. The answer lies in **value**.

If the price is within your financial limits and the animal meets your requirements without any other problems, then that horse represents good value. It is worth paying the full price for a sound animal that will be useful to you. You have not got value if the horse cost very little but was not capable of doing the work you intended. In addition, you should also remember that the animal will cost as much to equip and keep whether it costs £500 or £5000. Furthermore, there is no such thing as a fixed price—haggling is perfectly acceptable. Cash terms can encourage discounts but beware of handing over the money until you are sure about *all* aspects of the purchase, remember the legal phrase *caveat emptor* (i.e. let the buyer beware).

## Saying 'No'

The majority of horses and ponies that you look at in adverts and at yards will not be suitable for the purposes you intend and can be dismissed out of hand. You will be able to reduce the number of promising candidates to a very small number.

If the animal does not feel right or you're unhappy with the vendor or any other part of the deal, then walk away. Don't be persuaded by a skilled sales person to make a decision that you will regret.

## Ownership

A question that should be asked, but in many cases is overlooked, is whether the animal actually belongs to the seller. Proof of ownership can be difficult. Bear this in mind, especially in view of the large number of horse thefts that occur every year. If a freeze brand mark is evident, it can be worth asking to see the registration papers—if not available, ask why. It may be possible to approach the companies that provide a freeze branding service to see if that animal has been reported as stolen. More recently, 'Identichips' (small microchips inserted into the neck) have become available for use in horses— again it can be worth enquiring whether such a chip has been used since there will not be any external sign to suggest that is the case.

*Golden Rule: Don't become too attached, too soon; wait until any potential problems have been ruled out.*

# Chapter 4

# Limiting the choice

> **Management checks**
>
> **Health checks**
>
> **Riding checks**
>
> **Veterinary checks**

## Management checks

Whenever you look at any potential purchase, you should always seek to see that animal in its normal environment. Some problems are only apparent when the horse is in the stable (see Chapter 9 about vices)— it may be that during the summer the horse is turned out all day so you don't get to see the problems.

Some problems are more apparent at certain times of year and vendors can elect to sell the animal during a less troublesome period—for example, 'sweet itch', an allergy to the bite of a small midge, is a problem seen during the warmer months when the midge is present in large numbers but the signs may be virtually undetectable during the winter.

You should be very wary of any vendor who appears to try and hide *any* aspect of management (e.g. stabling, boxing, grooming, picking out feet, shoeing, etc.). Make a written note of any behaviour or features that appear unusual to you. It is always helpful to have a knowledgeable friend to advise in the early stages, but remember, a little knowledge can be a dangerous thing. If possible, an unannounced visit to see the animal can be quite revealing since the vendor has no opportunity to hide or disguise things before your arrival—once again, be wary if you provoke an unusual response from the vendor.

## Health checks

A general health check can be readily carried out in a few minutes by following a simple routine such as that outlined in Appendix 1.

A number of pertinent questions you may also care to ask are included there.

## Riding check

As mentioned in the previous chapter, ensure that you have ridden the animal before proceeding further to eliminate animals that are totally unsuitable for you because of the ride.

## Veterinary checks

Having found a horse that passes your own scrutiny, now is the time to consider having a prior to purchase examination by a vet. Any possible problems that you may have discerned should be mentioned to your vet when you arrange a vetting. Your vet may be able to advise whether they could jeopardise the purchase. The significance of some problems may only become apparent at the time of the examination.

*Golden Rule: Learn as much as possible about the animal you are looking at before committing yourself to any purchase.*

# Chapter 5

# Should I use a vet?

**The vet's role**

**Responsibility for fees**

**Vetting**

**Costs**

**Making a decision**

**Vendors certificates**

**What next?**

## The vet's role

Many of the commonest causes of discontent following purchase could be easily avoided by having a horse examined by a vet before purchase is completed. You should consider a vet as analogous to the surveyor who surveys your house before you buy. It is asking an expert to give an opinion on the suitability of the animal for the purpose you intend.

You will often hear the term 'sound' used to describe a horse or pony. The term refers not only to soundness of limb (i.e. that the horse is not lame) but also to all other aspects of the horses body which could affect that animal's usefulness for work (e.g. breathing problems, impaired vision, heart defects, etc.).

While vets don't come cheap, they may save you considerable heartache and expense by ensuring that you avoid a bad buy. It is always unfortunate if you call a vet out and the horse fails the examination for one or more reasons. It becomes even more disappointing if further vettings also result in failure. The temptation can be not to have further vettings and to take a gamble with the next animal you look at. This should be avoided.

Try to learn as much as possible about the reasons for failure so that you can look out for similar problems in other potential purchases. In the earlier chapters, it was stated that you should learn as much about the animal as possible before having the vetting—the aim of this is to ensure that horses that will obviously fail the vetting will not be looked at. This will go a long way towards avoiding the problem of having to call the vet out on several occasions.

If you are aware of any potential problems, it is very useful to chat to the vet before the vetting is carried out. Remember, vets are busy people so don't expect a prolonged phone conversation—have the facts to hand and explain them as clearly as possible. If the problem described is likely to jeopardise the vetting, then the vet may well be able to tell you over the phone. Don't expect this in all cases or with all problems, since some can only be assessed at the time of the examination. Potential problems can also be brought to the vet's attention at the examination—a preliminary check by the vet may prevent the wasted cost of the rest of the vetting procedure if the problem turns out to be serious. Wherever possible, it is wise for you to be present at the vetting so vet can bring any problems that might be found to your immediate attention.

## Responsibility for fees

It is you, the purchaser, who is responsible for the vet fees whether the horse passes or fails. That said, the vet is there for *your* benefit, not the vendors. While the view of the vet should be impartial whether the vendor is a client of his/hers or not, it would perhaps be wise to use your own vet or a local horse vet who is not known to the vendor.

When considering whether to progress with a purchase, you should always enquire whether there is any objection to having the animal examined by a vet. If the vendor objects or starts making excuses, *do not proceed further*.

## Vetting—what is it?

A vetting or 'Examination of a horse on behalf of a purchaser' is a detailed examination carried out by a qualified vet.

Most vets will follow a specified procedure as laid out in a Joint Memorandum prepared by the Royal College of Veterinary Surgeons and the British Veterinary Association. This procedure follows a general routine of examination that is designed to detect clinical signs of injury or disease.

Most vets will be prepared to do one of two types of examination, the choice of which will depend on the purchase price of the animal and the use for which it is intended:

**Full vetting**

This is a very comprehensive examination that will take in the region of two hours to complete. The examination is carried out in five stages, followed by the issuing of a certificate:

*(1) Preliminary examination*

This is a thorough examination of the horse or pony which will include looking at its teeth to give guidance as to age.

*(2) Trotting-up*

The animal is walked and trotted on hard level ground to ensure that it is sound at this stage (i.e. free from lameness).

*(3) Strenuous exercise*

The aim here is to exert the animal, not to exhaust it. The exercise should be sufficiently vigorous to make the animal breathe deeply, to increase the action of the heart, and to reveal strains or injuries by stiffness or lameness after a period of rest. Riding horses are ridden at canter for about 5-10 minutes, and then a controlled gallop is carried out. If the horse is too young or untrained, then the strenuous exercise should be carried out by lunging.

*(4) A period of rest*

The horse is allowed to stand quietly in the stable for about half an hour. The breathing is observed and the heart is checked.

*(5) The second trot and foot examination*

The horse is examined again as in stage 2. The horse is also made to walk backwards a few strides and to turn in tight circles. If there are doubts about the condition of the feet, permission to remove the shoes may be sought from the vendor.

● *Certification*

Having completed the five part examination, the vet will discuss the findings in full with the purchaser. A certificate will be produced to certify what was found by way of disease, injury or physical abnormality and the vet will express an opinion on whether the animal is suitable for purchase for the purpose intended.

● *Exceptions*

Certain factors are not considered by the routine examination outlined above. For example, the certificate does not cover an examination for pregnancy (such an examination could be carried out at special request), and the height of the pony or horse is not the concern of the vet (though again a request to bring a measuring stick could be made). Vices (see Chapter 9) are objectionable habits but may not always be found during the examination. As stated on the 'Prior to purchase examination certificate', if you wish to obtain a warranty covering such matters as height, freedom from vices, the non-administration of drugs prior to examination (e.g. to hide a lameness or to quieten a fractious animal), or the animal's existing performance as a hunter, show jumper, riding pony, eventer, etc., then you should do so in writing from the vendor (see Chapter 6). It is not the responsibility of the vet to provide or seek this cover.

● *Blood samples*
A vet can and will, on request, take a routine blood sample at the time of the examination that can be tested for drugs routinely at extra cost; alternatively and perhaps more likely, it can be stored for a period of two to three weeks and, should a problem arise shortly after purchase (e.g. lameness), the sample can be tested. Drugs that can be detected include phenylbutazone ('bute') used to mask lameness, clenbuterol (Ventipulmin) used to mask breathing problems, and some sedative drugs (e.g. acetylpromazine) used to calm fractious animals. Any vendor that objects to a routine blood sample should be treated with great suspicion. Most have no objection since it can provide security to them as much as the purchaser should a query arise.

## Short (Part 1 & 2) vetting
In some cases the relatively low asking price for a horse or pony makes the cost of a full vetting prohibitive. Also, the nature of the work to be undertaken (e.g. light hacking) may be such that a full vetting is not strictly necessary.

In these cases, many vets will be prepared to carry out a so-called short vetting which is essentially the first two parts of the full vetting procedure outlined above. The initial examination is equally thorough and the basic soundness of limb is determined. This examination will not assess problems of lameness that may arise from strenuous exercise, nor problems of breathing or heart function related to exercise. Nonetheless, this short examination may prevent many bad purchase decisions being made.

# Costs

The cost of a vetting will vary from vet to vet and area to area. You are essentially paying for the vet's time and expertise. You should expect to pay a visit fee unless you actually take the horse to the vet— visit fees are usually influenced by the distance travelled. You should ask for an estimate of the cost of the vetting and the visit fee when you make the arrangements. You can also ask which type of vetting would be considered most appropriate.

## Making a decision

Following the examination, the vet will explain all the findings to you. He should be able to tell you whether any problems are sufficiently significant that the horse should not be bought. Not all the problems that a vet finds will be a cause of unsoundness—nevertheless, if the vet is concerned about these problems, his advice should be heeded since he will be speaking from practical experience. If an animal fails the vetting, it is worth discussing in detail why—it may be that you consider that you could live with the problem and that the vendor will accept a lower sum. (If the vet says definitely don't buy, then you would be strongly advised not to.)

Horses may fail vettings for one of any number of reasons. However, the common factor is that they may affect the animal's usefulness for the work intended by the purchaser in the near or distant future.

## Vendor's certificates

On occasions, a vendor may show you a vetting certificate for the animal you are considering buying. Such certificates should always be viewed with caution as even a recent certificate may rapidly become inaccurate. It is *always* safer to have your own vetting carried out.

## What next?

By this stage, you have now found an animal that meets all your riding requirements and which is considered to be a safe and sound purchase prospect. The temptation is to dive in and hand the cash over. Beware! Even at this stage you are strongly recommended to take things cautiously.

Firstly check through all the stages you have so far completed:

- ❐ Are you sure you are ready to accept the responsibility and commitment of horse ownership? It is not too late to back out with minimal financial loss.
- ❐ Consider again who is going to ride the animal and whether *all* of their requirements have been met. If not, stop now!
- ❐ Finance—run over the total costings again and make sure you are within your financial limits. Do not cause yourself financial embarrassment.
- ❐ Check all your own observations about the situation the animal is coming from, and check that you are satisfied with what you have been told by the vendor. Remember, not all vendors are Saints!
- ❐ Check the findings of the vet—if you are in any doubt about any aspect of the vet's report, then contact the vet and ask for an explanation. Vets provide professional opinion but even vets are human.

Right—all systems are nearly go! The next stage is to get some form of written warranty to protect your interests.

*Golden Rule: Always have a pony or horse examined by a vet prior to purchase.*

# Chapter 6

# Warranties

> **The need**
>
> **The content**
>
> **Legal advice**
>
> **Method of payment**
>
> **Vendor's identity**

Examination of an animal by a qualified vet before purchase is an extremely useful means of detecting potential causes of trouble at an early stage. However, the examination does have its limitations.

## The need for a warranty

It must be remembered that the vetting certificate will stipulate '...at the time of my examination...'. Problems that could not have been reasonably detected or determined at that time will not be covered, nor will problems that could have arisen since purchase. As mentioned in the earlier chapter on vettings, the examination does not include routinely an examination for pregnancy; it does not consider reproductive function; also some vices (behavioural problems) may not be detectable at the time of the vetting examination.

It is very much in the interest of the purchaser to obtain some kind of *written* warranty from the vendor. A warranty is a legal document that may be presented at a later stage should legal proceedings become necessary. It is essential, therefore, to ensure that the warranty is written in a clear, concise, non-ambiguous way.

## The content

A written warranty should essentially indicate that a horse is sound and free from vice. It is quite reasonable to ask that the warranty covers age, soundness of wind, limb and sight, freedom from vice, and suitability for the purpose for which you intend to use the animal. Some of these matters will also be covered by the vetting examination (e.g. age).

Alarm bells should ring in the mind of the potential purchaser if a vendor is reluctant to qualify any of the points mentioned. Any words used on the warranty should be clear cut and not open to alternative interpretation. For example, it is totally unacceptable to use a term such as 'believed sound'.

Details that should be included on the warranty document are as follows:

- The name and address of the vendor.
- The name and address of the buyer.
- The date of the agreement.
- A description of the animal concerned—this may include a brief description of markings as well as height, age, sex, freeze brand marks, etc.
- Actual terms of warranty e.g. 'warranty that this 10 y.o. bay gelding is sound, free from vice, and quiet to ride'.
- Exclusions i.e. any item not to be covered under warranty.
- The signature of the buyer, the vendor and, ideally, an independent witness.

## Legal advice

Remember that a warranty is a legal document and you would be well advised to seek a solicitor's advice in drawing up a warranty document if you have any doubts. The present Sale of Goods Act 1979 provides a certain amount of protection to the buyer when dealing with horse traders (i.e. people dealing in horses as a business), but such laws can be difficult to interpret when applied to live animals. Private sales, where no established business is involved, provide less protection to the purchaser. The objective of a written warranty is to minimise the scope for misrepresentation or misinterpretation (deliberate or otherwise) by the vendor. A written statement is undoubtedly preferable to word of mouth when legal matters are at stake.

## Method of payment

When deciding the terms of a warranty, it is also a useful time to agree in writing the terms of payment, ( deposit with trial, instalments, etc.).

Regardless of the method of payment, you should always obtain a written receipt *immediately* when any form of financial transaction takes place.

## Vendor's identity

**A cautionary note:** a warranty will only be of value if you can trace the person from whom you bought the animal. Remember what was said earlier about studying the vendor as well as the animal—many rogues are only too willing to sell you a duff horse and then quietly disappear.

> *Golden Rule: Always obtain some form of written warranty before completing a purchase of a horse or pony.*

# Chapter 7

# Ageing a horse or pony

**Identification**

**'Aged' horses**

**The need for expert advice**

**The 'right' age**

The true age of the animal is probably one of the greatest causes of dispute that follows the sale of a horse or pony. Such problems are entirely avoidable by following the recommendations in this guide, since protection is provided in the form of the vetting examination and also in the form of the warranty recommended in Chapter 6.

## Identification

When suitably accurate paper documentation of a horse's age is not available, (any document carrying the animal's age must also have a description of the animal to which it relates to be valid), then age is *estimated* by examination of the teeth. The rate of wear and precise eruption times of teeth do vary from animal to animal but are sufficiently consistent for the method to be useful.

## 'Aged' horses

As horses get older, the accuracy of ageing by this method becomes increasingly poor. Once beyond about twelve years of age, the horse will often be described as 'aged' because the teeth are worn to the point where accurate ageing is simply *not possible*. Many vets will use the term 'aged' in horses as young as eight years. The limitations of this method are therefore clear. **Do not be fooled by anyone who claims to accurately age old horses.**

# The need for expert advice

Ageing of horses is definitely not for the beginner. You will see pictures of horses' teeth in many books which show how they should look at various ages. Regrettably, the horses don't read the textbooks! Leave assessment of age to an expert, the most useful person being a vet since he/she can provide a veterinary certificate of ageing.

It was not unknown in the past for dishonest dealers to alter the marks on teeth to deceive unwary purchasers. This practice was termed 'bishoping'. Fortunately such cases are rarely encountered now but, despite that, many people are duped into buying a supposedly 8-10 year old horse which in reality is the best part of 15-25 years old.

Don't be fooled by the large number of supposedly 8-10 year old horses that are for sale. It is an old dealers' joke that 'all horses are nine', but it is no laughing matter to be on the receiving end of such a confidence trick. Remember too that external appearances can be deceiving—a neglected animal can look old before its time, while a well-kept pony or horse can look much younger than its true age.

## The 'right' age

The age of horse you should buy depends very much on your experience as a rider and the type of animal you are seeking. Horses are generally mature and ready to work at four years old and do their best work between five and seventeen years of age. The peak years are considered to be nine to thirteen years of age. These are generalisations since there are many sound, fit horses and ponies working well into their twenties (and even their thirties!).

A young horse may need a lot of work to bring it on and thus may not really be suitable for a beginner/novice rider. Conversely, excessive maturity may severely restrict the usefulness and working life expectancy of an animal, and may severely limit its resale value. While resale value may not be at the front of your mind when buying a horse, it is an important point to consider since the animal can be an expensive investment. A change in your personal circumstances may force a sale—it is better to buy an animal that will enable you to recoup the bulk of your outlay should the need arise.

*Golden Rule: Leave the ageing of horses and ponies to experts.*

# Chapter 8

# Conformation

Many people will refer to the 'conformation' of a horse and the amount of 'bone' a particular animal has. The subject of conformation is very complex but it essentially refers to the shape and form of an animal. It is very important since the conformation of the animal may influence how well it functions, i.e. its suitability for work/exercise. Poor conformation may predispose the animal to problems sooner or later in life—poor conformation can put undue stress on particular parts of the body (especially the limbs).

## Significance

When you are buying a horse you are strongly recommended to find a horse with reasonably normal conformation. The perfect horse simply does not exist. An assessment of conformation will be made by the vet at the time of the vetting examination. While the conformation of a given animal may not, in itself, be an unsoundness, it may render a horse liable to problems that could give rise to unsoundness. It must, therefore, be considered as a potential reason to decline a purchase. The subject of conformation is a highly subjective area and can be a cause of considerable dispute between vendors, vets and purchasers.

## Abnormalities and advice

You will come across many terms describing abnormalities of conformation, e.g. pigeon-toed, splay footed, cow hocked, sickle hocked, camped behind, calf knees, buck knees, bow legs, bench knees, upright pastern, short pastern, long pastern and so on. Don't be overwhelmed—you really do not need to understand these terms unless you have a particular interest in the subject. What you need to know is whether the horse will be reasonably able to carry out the work you expect both in the short term and the long term. Leave the detailed assessment of conformation to an expert, but it is sometimes useful to find a friend who has some idea of reasonable shape so that obvious problem horses can be ruled out before the vet is called in.

## Assessment

When looking at a horse or pony, its general outline and shape should be pleasing to the eye and no obvious faults should be evident. You should examine the standing animal from all viewpoints (front, back and sides). You should also see the animal moving both in a walk and a trot, away from you and towards you. Some conformational faults will become very apparent during movement but may be far less obvious in the standing animal.

## Inches of bone

In some adverts, you may see the term '8 inches of bone' or '9 inches of bone' or similar. This refers to a measurement around the foreleg taken just below the knee. The amount of bone (which actually includes bone and tendon) is considered to influence the weight carrying capacity of the horse. For example, nine inches of bone may suggest the horse could reasonably carry up to fourteen stone. However, such measurements provide no hard and fast guarantees and commonsense must prevail!

*Golden Rule: The perfect horse or pony does not exist.*

# Chapter 9
# Vices

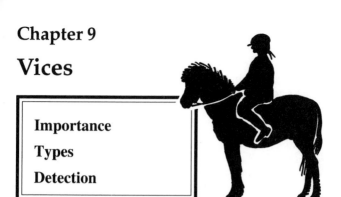

- Importance
- Types
- Detection

## Importance

A vice is an abnormal and objectionable behaviour which has become a habit in that individual. Such habits are extremely difficult to break and can be a constant source of irritation to the owner. Whenever you buy a horse, it is important to try and establish whether any vices exist.

## Types

There are many types of vice, some being more troublesome than others. They can be broadly divided into two main groups

- Vices associated with character or temperament
- Vices seen in housed animals.

Examples of these two groups are listed below:

### Character/temperament vices
This group includes:

- Aggressive behaviour to humans or other horses e.g. biting, kicking, pushing, striking out, barging.
- Rebellious behaviour against restraint or command by backing, bucking, rearing, head throwing, refusing to box, refusing to stand when mounted, bolting, etc.
- 'Cold backed'—horses which excessively resent being saddled, having the girth tightened, or being mounted.
- 'Rig-like' behaviour refers to a gelding that behaves like a stallion but has been properly castrated (as opposed to a true rig which is an animal that has a retained testicle).

**Stall Vices**

This group includes:

- Crib-biting where the front teeth are hooked over any projecting object, the neck is arched, and the horse pulls back enabling air to be swallowed. It causes excessive wear on the teeth, can make animals look very poor in condition, and can predispose bouts of colic (abdominal discomfort).
- Windsucking where air is swallowed without crib-biting.
- Wood chewing/biting/licking which can result in injuries to the mouth.
- Weaving where the horse stands at the box door and rocks from side to side.
- Pacing/box walking/circling—stereotyped behaviour seen in the box rather than at the box door.
- Pawing, kicking and knee knocking—these may or may not be associated with feeding times.
- Tail rubbing, bed eating and dung eating—these will be considered vices when no cause for the problem can be established (i.e. no nutritional deficiency or skin disease is present).

Some vices such as weaving and stall walking can be picked up by other horses or ponies in a yard if an affected animal is introduced.

# Detection

Every effort should be made to ascertain whether a horse that you are considering buying has any vices. You should observe the horse or pony on different occasions in a stall or loosebox. You should also watch the animal at pasture in the company of other horses and ponies.

In some cases the vendor will go to considerable amounts of trouble to avoid the circumstances under which a vice may be seen. Therefore, there is a great deal to be said for visiting a horse, unannounced to the owner, to observe the animal in its natural state. (Please note, this is not a license to trespass—you should obtain the owner's permission to look, the aim is to prevent any interference to the animal before you arrive).

Clipping, grooming, picking out feet and other routine procedures should be considered and where possible tried. Also try loading the animal in a box or trailer. Try catching the animal in an open field. It may also be worth seeing the horse shod since some animals can be difficult with farriers but normal otherwise.

*Golden Rule: Vices can be a major cause of problems—if you can avoid buying a horse with any vice, then do so.*

# Chapter 10

# Recapitulation

If you follow the advice outlined in this guide, you should find an animal that meets all of your requirements and which will provide you with many years of pleasure. You will also be in a strong position when you come to sell the animal since you will know a great deal about the animal you have bought. Remember the key word when looking for a horse or pony is **value**, i.e. that you find an animal that meets your personal requirements within your financial means. You will find a good value animal by using common sense and not being in too much of a rush. A fool is easily parted from his money—don't be the fool!

In summary, the ten commandments when buying a horse or pony are:

1.  Be completely aware of *all* the implications of ownership.
2.  Set a comprehensive budget and stick to it—the purchase price of the animal is only one part of the total cost.
3.  Learn by reading, discussion and , if possible, observation, about the common types of problem seen in horses and ponies so you are not totally 'green' when you start looking.
4.  Look at several animals and don't be in a rush to buy.
5.  Try and establish the history of each animal you are looking at, but don't be gullible and don't believe everything you are told.
6.  Don't overestimate your own abilities in matters in which you are not expert—always get a vet to check before any final decision is made.
7.  Be prepared to haggle for the best possible price— there is no such thing as a fixed price when it comes to animals, and remember that any money saved in the purchase price can be used to help pay for tack, insurance, etc.

8.  Consider resale value since you may not keep the animal for the rest of its life.
9.  Always get things down in writing.
10. When it comes to the buying and selling of horses and ponies, trust nobody, not even your best friend!

In conclusion, it is worth remembering that a wrong decision in choosing which animal to buy can be emotionally and financially very upsetting. If you follow the advice given in this guide, you will successfully negotiate the minefield of problems that you may encounter when purchasing a horse or pony. And you will obtain in full the pleasure that can come from horse ownership.

*Golden Rule:* **Value** *in the form of financial and personal satisfaction is the aim at the end of the day.*

# Appendix 1
## Health check list

When viewing any horse or pony for the first time, there is a good opportunity to assess the animal's general health. Make sure nothing is missed by following a simple check list such as that outlined below:

## Manner

- ❐ The animal should be bright and alert, taking a keen interest in what is going on around.

## Head

- ❐ The ears should be pricked and mobile.
- ❐ The eyes should be bright, clean and wide open.
- ❐ The nostrils should be clean and free from discharge.
- ❐ Check for lumps, swellings and scars (particularly under the jaw).
- ❐ Part the lips and check that the upper and lower incisor (front) teeth meet properly. Beware if the upper teeth are too far forward ('parrot mouthed') or if the lower teeth are too far forward.
- ❐ Appetite should be good and the animal should show no difficulty chewing different types of food.

## Neck and body

- ❐ The mane and tail should be full—feel base of mane and tail for thickened skin or scabbiness (could be due to rubbing and irritation caused by allergy to biting midges often called 'sweet itch').
- ❐ The coat should be bright and clean and skin should be smooth and supple.
- ❐ The skin should be free from wounds, swellings and soreness.
- ❐ The animal should be neither too thin nor too fat.

## Legs and feet

- ❐ The animal should be comfortable and weight bearing on all four feet—resting a hind leg is not unusual but resting a front leg is very unusual.

- ❐ Check for heat, swellings and scarring especially over joints and tendons.
- ❐ The feet should be in good condition, the hoof wall free from cracks, the underside of the foot (the sole and frog) should be clean and healthy and not smelly.
- ❐ The shoes should be in good condition, properly fitted and show even signs of wear.

## Other points to note

- ❐ Breathing should be shallow and almost imperceptible at rest and increases (in rate and depth) with exercise. The normal breathing rate at rest is 8-12 breaths per minute.
- ❐ Heart rate or pulse is normally 32-40 beats per minute.
- ❐ Rectal temperature is normally 99-100.5°F (37.6-38.2°C).
- ❐ Dung should be well formed, not sloppy (though animals on lush grass may be rather less firm than normal).

## Questions to ask

- ❐ Vaccination history: Is the animal vaccinated against tetanus and equine influenza? If so, when was the last injection (booster) given and is there a record card signed by a veterinary surgeon?
- ❐ Does the animal have any form of registration papers e.g. breed society registration, freeze brand documents?
- ❐ What worming programme has been used and when was the horse/pony last wormed?
- ❐ What type and what quantity of feed is being offered?
- ❐ Is the vendor aware of any disease or injuries the animal has sustained? Many vendors will not be very forthcoming with such information. If not, does the vendor have any objections to the horse being examined by a vet or to a blood sample being taken as part of the examination procedure?

# Appendix 2
# Landmarks of the horse

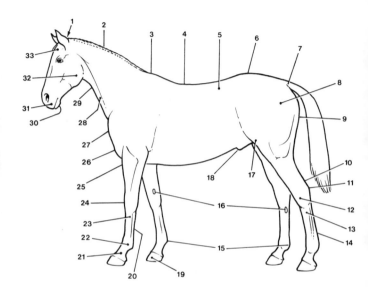

| | | |
|---|---|---|
| 1. Poll | 12. Hock joint | 23. Fore cannon |
| 2. Crest | 13. Hind cannon | 24. Knee |
| 3. Withers | 14. Flexor tendons | 25. Forearm |
| 4. Back | 15. Ergot | 26. Breast |
| 5. Loins | 16. Chestnuts | 27. Point of shoulder |
| 6. Croup | 17. Stifle joint | 28. Jugular groove |
| 7. Dock | 18. Sheath | 29. Windpipe |
| 8. Hip joint | 19. Coronet | 30. Chin |
| 9. Buttock | 20. Flexor tendons | 31. Muzzle |
| 10. Hamstring | 21. Pastern | 32. Cheek |
| 11. Point of hock | 22. Fetlock joint | 33. Forehead |

# Appendix 3
# Worms and worming

Horses grazing pasture may become infected with large burdens of internal parasites (worms). Control of these is based on repeated treatments with broad spectrum wormers throughout the year. The frequency of treatment is indicated by the life cycle of the worms; every 6-8 weeks is usually suggested. High stocking rates and limitations on available pasture may increase the severity of infection considerably thus necessitating more frequent treatment. Good pasture management, including picking up dung daily, is an essential component of a worm control programme which should not rely only on the worming treatments.

Infestation with worms may give rise to colic, diarrhoea, poor coat condition, anaemia and weight loss although in many instances no signs are present. The absence of symptoms should never be taken as an indication of freedom from worm infection.

There are many different types of 'worms', the table below lists some names and indicates where they can be found in the horse:

| Worm type | Where found |
|---|---|
| Large redworms (strongyles) | Large bowel |
| Migratory strongyles | Blood vessels of the bowel |
| Small redworms (strongyles) | Large bowel |
| Large roundworms | Small intestine |
| Threadworms | Small intestine |
| Pinworms | Large intestine, rectum |
| Lungworms | Respiratory tract |
| Tapeworms | Small and large intestine |

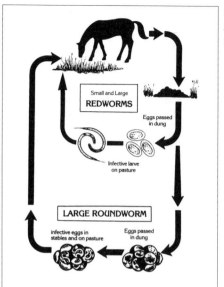

*Figure 1*
*Life cycle of the roundworm*

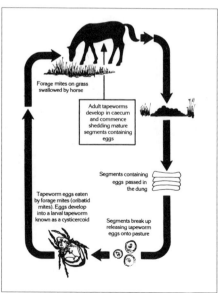

*Figure 2*
*Life cycle of the tapeworm*

# Appendix 4
# Glossary of terms

Many conditions can affect the suitability of an animal for purchase. The following conditions represent a few that are commonly seen in practice and which may be apparent during a preliminary examination or during a pre-purchase examination carried out by a veterinary surgeon.

*Arthritis*  Inflammation of a joint that can result in damage and change to cartilage and bone leading to lameness. It can be caused by injury, infection or excessive work.

*Bog spavin*  Swelling of the hock joint which may or may not be associated with other problems in the joint.

*Bone spavin*  Arthritic changes in the lower joints of the hock, a common cause of hind leg lameness.

*Broken wind*  Also known as *Heaves* or *COPD* (Chronic Obstructive Pulmonary Disease), this is usually the result of a chronic (long-standing) allergy to dust, and affected animals show very laboured breathing.

*Bursae*  Sacs containing synovial fluid found at points where tendons run over joints or bony prominences to minimise friction. They may become swollen if knocked, strained or damaged, e.g. capped elbow, capped hock, fetlock windgalls.

*Capped elbow*  Painless swelling usually resulting from injury by the foot when lying down, although it may be caused by friction on the ground during rising where insufficient bedding is provided.

*Capped hock*  Painless swelling over the hock usually resulting from injury by the foot when lying down or by the horse kicking the walls of the stall or loose box.

*Corns*  Bruising of the sole near the heels, most usually caused by poor fitting shoes or shoes being left on for too long.

| | |
|---|---|
| *Curb* | A thickening of the ligament running down the back of the hock joint (the plantar ligament) a few inches below the point of the hock. Usually caused by strain or the result of poor conformation. Can cause lameness. |
| *Epistaxis* | A nose bleed. Can be seen after hard exercise (a so-called 'broken blood vessel') or may result from trauma or disease in the head region. |
| *Galls & sores* | Caused by rubbing, e.g. girth galls, saddle sores, and usually due to poorly fitting saddlery. |
| *Hoof cracks* | Cracks starting at the ground surface are called grass cracks while those starting at the coronet (the top part of the hoof wall) are called sand cracks. Sand cracks tend to be a more serious problem since they can be caused by damage to the area from where the new hoof grows. |
| *Laminitis* | Inflammation of the sensitive tissues (laminae) under the wall of the hoof, most commonly caused by overeating (e.g. too much grass). It can lead to a flat or dropped sole due to rotation of the coffin bone in the foot. |
| *Mud fever* | An infection of the skin around the pastern area caused by a bacterium called Dermatophilus, and a variety of other infectious agents. Brought about by persistent exposure to mud and water which causes an inflammatory response. |
| *Napping* | Where the animal refuses to carry out commands from the rider. |
| *Navicular disease* | A complicated condition affecting a small bone in the foot. It is a common cause of chronic lameness. |
| *Quidding* | Where inefficient chewing causes food to be spilled. May be controlled by teeth rasping. |
| *Rainscald* | A bacterial infection in the skin caused by Dermatophilus bacteria (the same organism that causes mud fever), usually found on the back due to wet conditions. |

| | |
|---|---|
| *Ringbone* | Bony arthritic changes in and around the pastern and coffin joints, a common cause of lameness usually caused by trauma or age related wear and tear. |
| *Ringworm* | A contagious fungal infection of the skin. |
| *Roarer* | A respiratory noise heard during exercise caused by paralysis of (usually) the left side of the larynx. In mild cases there may be just a whistling noise during exercise. |
| *Sarcoids* | Benign skin tumours, one or more may be present. Can cause problems if they become large or occur in awkward places such as around the eyes. |
| *Sidebone* | Calcification (hardening) of the lateral cartilages of the foot. Not usually a major cause of lameness. |
| *Splint* | A small bony thickening formed between the splint bone and cannon bone, usually due to trauma or jarring. May cause lameness during formation but not usually a long-term problem. |
| *Thoroughpin* | Swelling of the tendon sheath around the deep flexor tendon near the point of the hock. Not usually a cause of lameness. |
| *Thrush* | Infection of the frog area of the foot, usually due to poor foot hygiene |
| *Windgalls* | Unsightly soft puffy swellings occur behind and just above the fetlock joint, mostly in the hind legs. They are not usually associated with lameness. |
| *Wolf tooth* | The vestigial remains of the first molar tooth, found just in front of the first proper cheek tooth. Not found in all horses and ponies. |

# Appendix 5
# Insuring your horse or pony

As with any expensive or valuable item it is wise to insure against loss or damage. This applies as much to a horse or pony and associated equipment as it does to a house and its contents. Careful consideration should be given to the type of insurance cover that is most suited to your particular circumstances. The type of cover provided can vary widely from simple third party liability through to a fully comprehensive policy providing additional cover for veterinary fees, loss of use of the animal, death through accident or misadventure, and theft. Remember also to insure tack and other equipment as well as trailers or boxes—there is a massive and thriving industry in stolen horse equipment as well as the animals themselves.

There are many companies offering policies designed for horse owners. Some of these specialise in pet insurance while others will be better known as companies insuring cars, houses and other valuables. You should approach several companies and compare in detail the different policies that each has to offer. Ask other horse owners what their experiences have been with certain companies. **Read all the details** of the various policies—this obvious point is often ignored but many policies that appear suitable at first glance carry specific exclusions that may only be 'discovered' when a problem arises and a claim becomes necessary. Don't be caught out and remember when comparing costs to compare like with like!

At the present time, some companies do not insist on a veterinary examination prior to the acceptance of an application for cover. This situation may well change if insurance premiums are to be kept within acceptable levels. A veterinary examination may be required if the value attached to an animal rises beyond a certain level. Notwithstanding this, it is important that you do not knowingly fail to disclose any potential problems with the animal concerned to the company since this may invalidate the cover. Indeed, it may even render you liable to prosecution since non-disclosure is regarded as fraudulent. Clearly, an insurance company will not provide cover for a problem that is in existence prior to the inception of the policy, one of the commonest such problems being any form of lameness. A veterinary examination prior to purchase can be of great assistance in establishing the health of the animal prior to acceptance of a policy; it will reduce the likelihood of a company questioning the validity of a claim should a problem arise shortly after purchase.

When insuring an animal following purchase, it is important to ascertain exactly when the cover comes into effect. Many problems can arise in the period immediately after purchase. It should be established whether cover is provided during transportation to the new home. Injuries arising from fighting when a new horse or pony is introduced to a group are unfortunately quite common —check that you have cover for veterinary fees or other costs arising from such accidents.

You should consult carefully with the insurance company or broker you are dealing with before signing any binding agreement. Make sure you read the policy document carefully as soon as it is available. Clear up any queries immediately—you can avoid much distress and anguish at a later stage by taking this simple action.

# Appendix 6
# Suggested further reading

## General reading

*The Handbook of Riding* by Mary Gordon-Watson (Pelham Books).

*The Manual of Horsemanship* The official manual of The British Horse Society and The Pony Club. 9th Edition.

*The Manual of Stable Management* Series produced by The British Horse Society.

    Book 1 The Horse

    Book 2 Care of the Horse

    Book 3 The Horse at Grass

    Book 4  Saddlery

    Book 5 Specialist Care of the Competition Horse

    Book 6 The Stable Yard

    Book 7 Watering and Feeding.

*The Ultimate Horse Book* by Elwyn Hartley Edwards (Dorling Kindersley)—a good book for looking at the different breed types.

*The MacDonald Encyclopaedia of Horses*—looks at different breeds throughout the world and the uses to which they are put.

*Summerhays' Encyclopaedia for Horsemen.* Compiled by R.S. Summerhays and revised by Valerie Russell (Threshold Books)—a useful source of definitions for unfamiliar terms used in the horseworld.

## Feeding

*Feeding Your Horse and Pony* by Diana Tuke (J.A. Allen)—a practical no-nonsense guide to feeding.

# Health Matters

*The Horse Owner's Veterinary Handbook* by Tony Pavord & Rod Fisher (The Crowood Press).

*Understanding Your Horse's Health: A Practical Guide* by Janet Eley (Ward Lock).

*Veterinary Notes for Horse Owners* by Capt. M. Horace Hayes. Recently extensively revised and updated. Editor Peter Rossdale. (Stanley Paul).

# Riding Establishments

*Where to Ride 1992-93: A guide to B.H.S. Approved establishments in UK and Ireland* British Horse Society (Kenilworth Press).